ANTARCTICA

A NEW ARENA FOR GREAT POWER RIVALRY

Timurlenk Chekovikj

ISBN: 9798851280481

Imprint: Independently published

Catalog

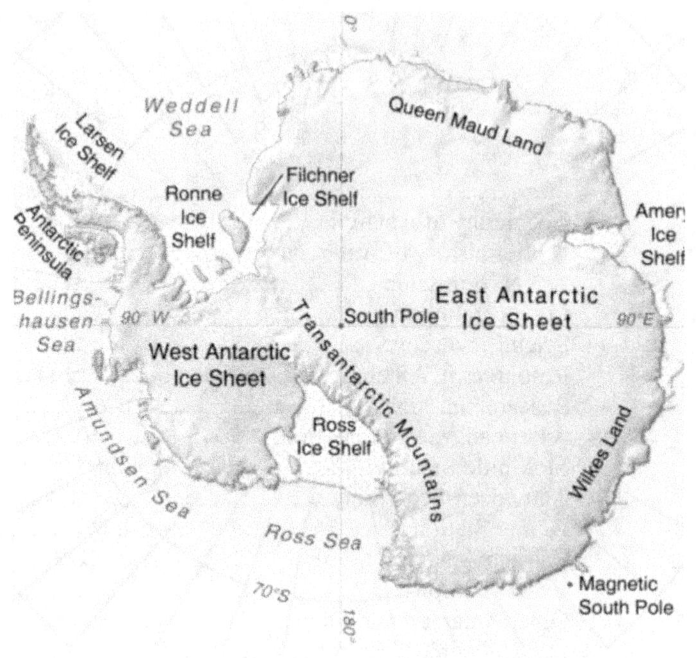

0°
Weddell Sea
Queen Maud Land
Larsen Ice Shelf
Filchner Ice Shelf
Ronne Ice Shelf
Antarctic Peninsula
Amery Ice Shelf
Bellings-hausen Sea
90° W
East Antarctic Ice Sheet
South Pole
90° E
West Antarctic Ice Sheet
Transantarctic Mountains
Amundsen Sea
Ross Ice Shelf
Wilkes Land
Ross Sea
70°S
180°
Magnetic South Pole

Intro

Antarctica is the coldest, driest, highest (on average), darkest and most uninhabited continent on Earth. Temperatures of -89.2 °C, and wind with a speed of 284 km/h were recorded, as well as a temperature drop of 36 °C in just 12 minutes.

At the South Pole, the ice is 2700 meters thick, and under that ice are other parts of the continent where there are mountains bigger than the Alps, and fresh water lakes bigger than Lake Ohrid.

The height of the air pressure and mountain peaks is almost like that of the Andes (average 3350 m) and the total humidity of the air is lower than that of the Sahara desert.[Report of the US Antarctic program. Washington DC 2012.]

In many places, water is only available in the form of ice. Dry weather and wind are ideal factors for causing fires. Antarctica represents the most challenging place for logistical support on Earth.

But that didn't stop people in the 19th century from starting a detailed research of this continent, completely unknown and undiscovered by people until then. In the 20th century, the "Antarctic Revolution" takes place and the South Magnetic Pole is conquered for the first time.

In fact, the idea of a vast southern land, called Terra Australis, had been speculated since ancient times, but it was not until the Age of Exploration that European sailors began to search for it The first confirmed sightings of the Antarctic mainland occurred in 1820, by three different expeditions: a Russian one led by Fabian Gottlieb von Bellingshausen and Mikhail Lazarev, a British one captained by Edward Bransfield, and an American one commanded by Nathaniel Palmer The first landing on the continent is attributed to the American sealer John Davis in 1821.

In the 20th century, the "Antarctic Revolution" takes place and the South Magnetic Pole is conquered for the first time. This refers to the period known as the Heroic Age of Antarctic Exploration, which spanned from the end of the 19th century to the end of World War I. During this time, many expeditions from various countries ventured into the Antarctic region, driven by scientific curiosity, national pride, and personal ambition. They made significant discoveries and achievements in geography, geology, biology, meteorology, and magnetism. One of the most notable feats was the race to reach the geographic South Pole, which was won by the Norwegian explorer Roald Amundsen and his team on December 14, 1911. They beat their British rival Robert Falcon Scott by five weeks, but Scott and his companions perished on their return journey. Other famous explorers of this era include Ernest Shackleton, Douglas Mawson, James Clark Ross, and Richard E. Byrd.

Antarctica is a place where thousands of scientists and tourists are visiting and exploring, looking with adoration into this challenge that remains in the legacy of generations to come. Uncertainty which awaits Antarctica in the 21st century is one of the largest in the history of mankind. Once we spend the reserves of oil, gold, copper, diamonds, it is an issue of a time when all arrangements for maintaining peace in the Antarctic will be replaced by a fight for territory and resources. Humanity can again be found in front of a new war. This war will be determined by scientific advances, economic interest and political change.

Antarctica is governed by a unique international treaty system that was established in 1959, at the height of the Cold War. The Antarctic Treaty System (ATS) sets aside the continent as a scientific preserve, where military activity is banned and freedom of scientific investigation is guaranteed. The treaty also suspends all territorial claims and disputes, and prohibits any activities related to mineral resources, except for scientific research. The treaty has been signed by 54 countries, representing about two-thirds of the world's population.

However, the treaty is not permanent and may be modified or amended by the parties. Some experts have raised concerns that the treaty may not be able to withstand the pressures of growing geopolitical and economic interests in the region, especially as climate change makes some resources more accessible. Antarctica is estimated to have vast reserves of oil, gas, coal, iron ore, copper, gold, nickel, and other minerals that could be worth trillions of dollars. Some countries may seek to exploit these resources or assert their territorial claims in the future, potentially leading to conflicts or violations of the treaty. Antarctica is a continent of peace, science and international cooperation.

However, it is also a continent of geopolitical interests, territorial claims and natural resources. In recent years, Antarctica has become a potential arena for competition and conflict among great powers, especially in the context of the ongoing Ukraine crisis.

The Ukraine crisis is a violent conflict that erupted in February 2022, when Russia invaded and annexed parts of eastern and southern Ukraine, violating its sovereignty and territorial integrity. The crisis has triggered a series of sanctions, counter-sanctions, diplomatic tensions and military confrontations between Russia and its allies on one side, and Ukraine and its supporters on the other side. The crisis has also raised concerns about the stability and security of Europe and the world order.

Therefore, it is crucial to maintain and strengthen the cooperation and trust among the parties to the treaty, and to ensure that Antarctica remains a place of peace and science for the benefit of all humanity.

Geography of Antarctica

Antarctica is the fifth largest continent on Earth, ahead of Europe and Australia. The geography of Antarctica is primarily dominated by ice, which represents 98% of its surface and only 2% is covered by rocky land. The continent of Antarctica is located in the Southern Hemisphere and is placed asymmetrically around the South Pole. It is surrounded by the southern waters of the world's oceans, from the South Pacific (Antarctic) Ocean, the Atlantic and the Indian Ocean. It covers an area slightly larger than 14 million km2.

With an average ice thickness of 1.6 km, under its surface there are entire lakes and rivers, the largest of which is Lake Vostok (26,000 km2) and the Onyx River (25 km). The highest point is the Vinson massif with a height of 4897 m. The lowest point is the Bentley Trench with a depth of over 2.5 km. The climate is subarctic and arctic, while the coast is 17,968 km long. Antarctica can be divided into two parts, West and East Antarctica. That division is conditioned by the Trans-antarctic Mountains.

East Antarctica is much larger, while West Antarctica can be said to be the warmer and more explored part of the continent. West Antarctica is covered by the West Antarctic ice sheet, which is quite sensitive and according to a large number of researchers, if it melts, it could lead to a rise in the global level of ocean waters up to several meters, which could cause major consequences in the world. However, if that process were to take place, it would take at least a century and would result in mass migrations of peoples because large human populations are concentrated along the coasts.

East Antarctica is covered by the East Antarctic ice sheet, which is more stable and thicker than its western counterpart. It also contains several active volcanoes, some of which are buried under the ice One of them is Mount Erebus, which is the highest active volcano in Antarctica and the southernmost active volcano on Earth. It has been erupting continuously for decades, producing lava lakes and ice fumaroles. Another one is Deception Island, which is actually the caldera of an active submarine volcano. It has erupted several times in the 20th century, destroying scientific stations and endangering wildlife. Other volcanoes in East Antarctica include Mount Berlin, Mount Discovery, Mount Frakes, and Gaussberg.

The presence of volcanoes in East Antarctica poses some challenges and opportunities for scientific research. On one hand, they create hazards for human activities and infrastructure, as well as environmental impacts such as ash emissions and glacial melting. On the other hand, they offer unique insights into the geology, geophysics, geochemistry, and biology of this remote region. They also provide sources of geothermal energy that could be used for heating and power generation[United States National Science Foundation]

A brief history of Antarctic research

Terra Incognita or unknown land is the last continent of the earth in which large areas are still unexplored. Antarctica is the last continent of the earth in which large areas are still unexplored. For centuries, people speculated about the existence of a vast southern land, called Terra Australis, but it was not until the Age of Exploration that European sailors began to search for it. The first Antarctic landmass to be discovered was the island of South Georgia by the English navigator Anthony de la Roche in 1675.

In 1739, French navigator Lozier Bouvet was the first European to spot the Southern Islands off Antarctica, but he could not land there because of the dangerous icebergs.

The first complete circumnavigation of Antarctica recorded in history books was made by Captain James Cook in 1773, after which the "island" was forgotten until rediscovered in 1808 by the Englishman Lindsay.

The first confirmed sightings of the Antarctic mainland occurred in 1820, by three different expeditions: a Russian one led by Fabian Gortlieb von Bellingshausen and Mikhail Lazarev, a British one captained by Edward Bransfield, and an American one commanded by Nathaniel Palmer. It was officially confirmed and accepted that in 1820 the Russian mission led by Mikhail Lazarev and Fabian Gortlieb von Bellinghausen with the ships Mirny and Vostok rediscovered Antarctica.

The first landing on the continent is attributed to the American sealer John Davis in 1821. Several expeditions followed in the 19th century, mainly for commercial and cartographic purposes. They explored the sub-Antarctic islands and regions, hunted seals and whales, charted the coastlines and the magnetic field, and discovered new features such as the Ross Sea, the Ross Ice Shelf, and Victoria Land.

The following researches were carried out mostly by Germany, so in 1898 the German Imperial Expedition "Valdivia" cleared up the mystery of the island for which they determined that there is only one island, and not two as the previous expeditions thought .

The 20th century marked the beginning of the Heroic Age of Antarctic Exploration, a period of intense scientific and geographical exploration that lasted from 1895 to 1917. During this time, many expeditions from various countries ventured into the Antarctic region, driven by scientific curiosity, national pride, and personal ambition. They made significant discoveries and achievements in geography, geology, biology, meteorology, and magnetism. One of the most notable feats was the race to reach the geographic South Pole, which was won by the Norwegian explorer Ronald Amundsen and his team on December 14, 1911. They beat their British rival Robert Falcon Scott by five weeks, but Scott and his companions perished on their return journey. Other famous explorers of this era include Ernest Shackleton, Douglas Mawson, James Clark Ross, and Richard E. Byrd.

Here we should also mention the unsuccessful missions of Otto Nordenskjöl's ship "Antarctica", which sank in the Weddell Sea. A similar fate awaited the German ship Deutchland, which barely survived the difficult weather. In 1915, Ernest Shackleton's ship sank in the Weddell Sea, and the expedition barely survived until they were rescued by a whaling ship that came after them. In the month of May, 1926 , for the first time , Richard Byrd claims to have flown over the South Pole with a Foker F-VII airplane, which will later be denied by numerous scientists and researchers. However, in the period 1928-1930, Richard Byrd with two ships and three planes will carry out a mission that will place him in the history of scientific research. In 1932 the British expedition Discoveri II was almost lost. Antarctica is a place that does not reveal its secrets easily to anyone

The Nazi mission

The greatest authority in collecting data about Antarctica in the time before the Second World War was the Germans. Because of this, the Nazis themselves organized the most sophisticated Antarctic research at that time in 1938-39.

Still, that mission is shrouded in secrecy and it is not clear why Hitler put so much effort into sending a mission to Antarctica right before the start of World War II. That expedition was the Deutche Antarktische Expedition, 1938-1939. The patron of this operation was personally Hermann Göring, the commander-in-chief of the German Air Force. With that, for the first time, in addition to the naval forces, the air forces of the German "Luftwaffe" are included in the research missions, which made photographic maps and reconnaissance of the Antarctic terrain. For the first time, a large part of Antarctica was declared a German country under the name Neu-Schwabenland, and the ship was called Schwabenland, which carried two planes and launched us with the help of a catapult. Germany publicly announced about that new colony of hers , and it did not meet special interest from the Great Powers at that time.

The German Nazi mission was very well equipped with material and technical means and also brought with it numerous experts from various scientific fields as well as numerous technicians. Since it was a military mission it contained discipline and the mission itself was a military secret. What was found during that mission is still not fully known, but in 1947, Admiral Richard Byrd carried out a massive military intervention in Antarctica and chased after the remaining German submarines. Operation Highjump represents the largest mission ever conducted in Antarctica with one aircraft carrier, 13 ships, 6 helicopters and 20 other aircraft involved. The total number of personnel amounted to over 4000 people.

It should be noted that the German Nazi mission successfully activated military bases in the Antarctic and Arctic regions and all this lasted until the end of the Second World War, where it was realized that the American fleet had to be fully engaged to suppress the numerous guerrilla bases especially in the Arctic region and Greenland.

Apart from a few captured and a few abandoned bases, the US fleet did not managed to fully detect the whereabouts of the German bases, although in doing so it used enormous resources to conquer the vast space.

Although Operation Highjump was not a classic military mission, it represented the first major military engagement , thus indicating the attention and importance that Antarctica has for America, as well as the role of other great powers and its geopolitical determination.

Living conditions

Living conditions in Antarctica are extremely harsh, temperatures vary from -80°C and -90°C in the interior in winter to +5°C and +15°C along the coast in summer. That's why the Antarctic is colder than the Arctic.

The Antarctic is colder than the Arctic for several reasons. One of them is that Antarctica is a landmass surrounded by ocean, while the Arctic is an ocean surrounded by landmasses. This means that Antarctica does not benefit from the moderating influence of the ocean, which can transfer heat from lower latitudes to higher ones. The ocean under the Arctic ice is cold, but still warmer than the ice or the air above it. So the ocean warms the air a bit in the Arctic, but not in Antarctica.

Another reason is that Antarctica has a much higher average elevation than the Arctic. Most of Antarctica is covered by a thick ice sheet that forms a huge plateau, rising up to 3 miles above sea level. The higher you go, the colder it gets, because the air pressure and density decrease with altitude. The air at high altitudes can hold less heat than the air at lower altitudes. The Antarctic ice sheet also reflects most of the sunlight that reaches it, reducing the amount of solar energy that can warm the surface.

A third reason is that Antarctica has stronger winds than the Arctic. These winds blow around the continent, creating a barrier that prevents warmer air from mixing with the polar air. This also happens in the Arctic, but to a lesser extent, because the winds surrounding the North Pole are not as strong or consistent. Therefore, warmer air from the mid-latitudes can sometimes reach and warm up the Arctic, but not Antarctica.

Because the surface repels all ultraviolet radiation, burns are often obtained. Solar radiation during summer is stronger than the equatorial area due to the longer duration of sunlight. Heavy snowfall in record time has been observed along the coast. At the very edges of the continent, strong catabatic winds are present, while in the interior, although it is colder, the winds are more moderate.

Scientific discoveries in Antarctica

Antarctica is home to more than 70 lakes that are located under the ice sheet and are therefore the source of many scientific discoveries. It is assumed that there is mixing of water between the large number of lakes. One of the discoveries is that the largest lake, Vostok, is supposed to have microbial life.

In 2007, NASA sent a team to Lake Untersee looking for extremophiles in the highly alkaline water. The frozen surface of the lake shares similarities with Jupiter's satellite Europa, and if life is found it would mean the possibility of life on this satellite as well.

Lake Untersee is the largest surface freshwater lake in the interior of the Gruber Mountains of central Queen Maud Land in East Antarctica. It is permanently covered with ice and has a pH between 9.8 and 12.1, making it one of the most alkaline lakes on Earth The lake also has very low primary production in the water column, but hosts abundant microbial communities that grow on the lake floor as stromatolites, which are layered structures formed by cyanobacteria and other microorganisms.

Extremophiles are organisms that can survive and thrive in extreme environments, such as high or low temperatures, pressures, salinity, or pH levels. They are of interest to astrobiologists, who study the origin, evolution, and distribution of life in the universe, because they may provide clues about the potential for life on other planets or moons.

In 2007, NASA funded an expedition to Lake Untersee to study its extremophiles and their adaptations to the harsh conditions. The team drilled through the ice and collected water and sediment samples from different depths of the lake. They also deployed underwater cameras and sensors to monitor the physical and chemical properties of the lake.

The team found that Lake Untersee has some similarities with Europa, one of Jupiter's moons, which is thought to have a global ocean of liquid water beneath a thick layer of ice. Both Lake Untersee and Europa have alkaline water, low nutrient levels, and high oxygen concentrations. Both also have geothermal activity that may provide energy and heat for life.

The team also discovered that Lake Untersee has a unique ecosystem that is dominated by cyanobacteria that can photosynthesize even under very low light levels. These cyanobacteria form large mats that cover most of the lake floor and produce oxygen that dissolves in the water. The team also found evidence of other types of microorganisms, such as archaea, bacteria, fungi, and algae, that live in association with the cyanobacterial mats or in the sediments below them.

The team concluded that Lake Untersee is a valuable natural laboratory for studying extremophiles and their potential role in astrobiology. They suggested that if life exists on Europa or other icy worlds, it may resemble the microbial communities found in Lake Untersee or other Antarctic lakes If life is found it will strengthen the arguments for the presence of extraterrestrial life in extremely cold and methane-rich environments. Scientists have so far found extremophiles in boiling water, in ice, in nuclear reactors, so it is assumed that it is not strange to find them in such environments.

In 2011, the US National Research Center published a report titled Future Scientific Opportunities in Antarctica and the Southern Ocean.[Future Science Opportunities in Antarctica and the Southern Ocean]

The report is focused on the latest discoveries and discoveries related to global changes. Findings related to global change include studies of the trends and causes and effects of climate change, such as rising sea levels and changes in ocean currents. Due to these types of research, the ozone hole was discovered as well as the reason why it was created and why it is spreading, which was followed by a ban on the use of chlorofluorocarbons. Detected as early as 1985, it indicates a steady spread attributed to the presence of chlorofluorocarbons or popularly called CFCs in the atmosphere that decompensate ozone into other gases.

Every year a large area of depleted ozone layer or so-called "ozone hole" expands over Antarctica. Some scientific studies indicate that all this causes an increased and accelerated melting of the ice.[Nature (Nature Publishing Group) 460 : 792–795.] The Antarctic polar vortex causes serious depletion of the ozone layer. Some scientific studies indicate that all this causes an increased and accelerated melting of the ice.

The Antarctic polar vortex is a large-scale circulation of winds that forms around the South Pole during the winter and spring. It isolates the air inside it from the rest of the atmosphere, creating very cold and stable conditions. These conditions favor the formation of polar stratospheric clouds, which provide a surface for chemical reactions that destroy ozone. Ozone is a molecule composed of three oxygen atoms that protects life on Earth from harmful ultraviolet radiation from the Sun.

The ozone-depleting reactions are triggered by chlorine and bromine atoms that come from human-made substances such as chlorofluorocarbons (CFCs) and halons. These substances were widely used in refrigeration, aerosols, and fire extinguishers until they were banned by the Montreal Protocol, an international treaty that came into force in 1989. However, because these substances have long lifetimes in the atmosphere, they still persist and reach the stratosphere, where they are broken down by sunlight and release chlorine and bromine atoms.

Starting from late August to early October, a large area

of depleted ozone layer or so-called "ozone hole" expands over Antarctica, reaching its maximum size in September or October. The ozone hole can cover an area of more than 20 million square kilometers (about twice the size of Europe) and reduce the ozone concentration by more than 90 percent in some regions. The ozone hole usually recovers by December, when the polar vortex breaks down and warmer air mixes with the polar air.

Some scientific studies indicate that the ozone hole has an impact on the climate and ice of Antarctica. The ozone hole affects the temperature, wind, and precipitation patterns in the region, creating a cooling effect on the surface and a warming effect on the lower stratosphere. The cooling effect tends to increase the sea ice extent around Antarctica by reducing the melting and enhancing the freezing of ice.

However, the warming effect tends to increase the melting of ice shelves and glaciers on land by weakening the westerly winds that block the warm ocean currents from reaching the coast. The melting of land ice contributes to sea level rise and changes in ocean circulation.

The recovery of the ozone layer is expected to reverse these effects in the future, but it may also bring new challenges. As the ozone hole heals, the polar vortex may weaken and allow more warm air to penetrate into Antarctica, causing warming and drying in some areas. This could reduce the sea ice extent and increase the melting of land ice, especially in West Antarctica and the Antarctic Peninsula, where some ice sheets are already unstable and vulnerable to collapse.

It has also been found that Antarctica is the fastest warming region in the last half century, which has led to a temperature rise of as much as 2.8°C. With the covering of 61% of the Earth's fresh waters in the form of ice, the melting of them would lead to an increase in the world water level by 66 meters, so that ¼ of the world's population, according to today's concentration, would be under water. The largest ice melt according to NASA occurred in 2005 when an area of ice nearly the size of California melted, resulting in a temperature rise of as much as 5° C. A study published in the Nature Geoscience journal in January 2013 identifies West Antarctica as the fastest-warming area of Earth. All of this points to rapid and extreme changes taking place in Antarctica and affecting the changes of the entire Earth. Currently, the biggest discoveries are happening and expected from the American Neutrino Observatory (IceCube Neutrino Observatory), which is located next to the South Pole itself.

Resources in Antarctica

Exploitation of resources implies their extraction from nature and often, further processing to obtain raw materials. This activity represents a significant factor in the economy of a country. Resources represent materials and raw materials that are extracted or obtained. They can be biological or non-biological, and can be used directly or with pre-treatment.

Certain resources like sunlight are present all over the planet, but most occur in small and scattered areas. Most of them have a limited amount, but there are also those that are unlimited (sun, air, geothermal energy). Most resources are finite, meaning they can dry up if not handled carefully.

According to origin, resources are divided into:

Biological resources - originating from the biosphere (living and organic material). Such are the forests and the animals and the materials obtained from them. Fossil fuels such as coal and oil are also included here because they are created by the decomposition of organic substances.

Non-biological resources - consisting of non-living and inorganic material: land, drinking water, air, heavy metals and ores such as gold, iron, copper, silver, etc.

Since the time of the first explorers, the wealth of Antarctic resources has attracted the attention of active industries. Along the coast of the continent and in the Trans-antarctic Mountains, pockets of coal have been discovered, formed by the decaying grass swamps that covered the area fifty million years ago. It is also the main mineral source of Antarctica. Other minerals such as iron, copper and nickel have also been found in areas such as the Prince Charles Mountains in East Antarctica, although not in quantities that would make mining companies too happy.

Other minerals such as iron, copper and nickel have also been found in areas such as the Prince Charles Mountains in East Antarctica, although not in quantities that would make mining companies too happy.

Antarctica is rich in mineral resources, but most of them are buried under thick ice sheets or inaccessible due to the harsh climate and remoteness of the continent. The most abundant mineral resource in Antarctica is coal, especially in the Trans-antarctic Mountains, where it was formed during the Permian and Triassic periods, when Antarctica was part of the supercontinent Gondwana. Coal deposits have been estimated to range from 45 to 203 billion tons, but they are of low quality and difficult to exploit.

Other minerals that have been discovered in Antarctica include iron, copper, nickel, gold, platinum, silver, lead, zinc, chromium, cobalt, molybdenum, tin, uranium, and antimony. These minerals are mostly concentrated in the Prince Charles Mountains in East Antarctica, where they are associated with Precambrian metamorphic rocks and granites. However, these minerals are not believed to be present in quantities or grades that would rival other continents, and their extraction and transport would be expensive and environmentally damaging.

Antarctica also has potential offshore resources of oil and gas, especially in the Ross Sea and Weddell Sea basins. These basins contain sedimentary rocks that may have trapped hydrocarbons generated from organic matter. However, there is no direct evidence of oil or gas reserves in Antarctica, as no wells have been drilled to test them.

Moreover, the exploration and exploitation of oil and gas in Antarctica would face many technical, economic, and legal challenges.

Mining in Antarctica is prohibited by the Protocol on Environmental Protection to the Antarctic Treaty, which came into force in 1998. The protocol bans any activity related to mineral resources, except for scientific research.

The protocol also states that it can be reviewed after 50 years (in 2048), and any changes would require the agreement of all parties. The protocol aims to protect Antarctica as a natural reserve devoted to peace and science, and to prevent any environmental impacts from mining activities.

The world's need for oil and gas is a major challenge for an environmentally clean Antarctica. Although there is no solid evidence, studies of the rocks have led many scientists to hypothesize that vast amounts of oil lie beneath the ice, especially in an area called the Weddell and Ross seas.

During the energy crisis of the 1970's several oil companies saw Antarctica as a solution to future oil shortages and they announced plans to extract oil from the continent. If this were achieved, now oil tankers would regularly visit Antarctica. But the Protocol on Environmental Protection to the Antarctic Treaty, which entered into force in 1998, signed by 32 countries, led to a complete ban on mineral mining on this continent. This agreement is signed for an indefinite period of time and can be terminated if all parties agree, with the fact that in 2048 there will be a revision of this agreement and it can be changed if ¾ of the signatories decide not to respect it.

The big oil companies are still staying away from trying to exploit the Antarctic oil, for which, apart from the strict regulations, there are also the huge costs for drilling and transporting the oil, which certainly makes it less economical. However, this is all a relative term in a world that experiences new technological discoveries every day and will mostly depend on the factor of oil shortage and the increase in the price of oil worldwide.

In Antarctica, scientists have discovered another very interesting object of research and resources that are quite inaccessible on other continents.

Antarctica is the best place to find meteors. Considering the huge price of the meteors, it can be speculated how much all this will interest the great powers in Antarctica. An Australian expedition first found a meteor in 1912 and since then over 25,000 meteors have been found, and the continent has been a meteor collector's paradise ever since.

They are easily noticeable on the "blue ice" and in areas that are permanently covered with ice, because the snow does not stay on those surfaces. Scientists have also discovered that meteorites hidden in Antarctic ice are much better preserved than other meteorites found anywhere on Earth, as the ice has protected them from rusting, decay, weathering and erosion. Some of the samples are 700,000 years old and some are supposed to be fragments from Mars. Meteors give us information about the origin of the composition of the Sun, Moon, Earth and other planets. But in addition to the value of scientific research, meteorites are of particular value to private and other collectors. Therefore, there is a justified fear that if the meteors end up in other hands, and not in scientific hands, many important scientific discoveries will remain beyond the reach of scientists.

Biological resources are also an important factor on the Antarctic continent. The hunting of whales and krill "shrimps" should also be included here. It is known that Antarctica is home to the "krill" population that counts several hundreds of billions of tons, which is the main food of whales, that is, it represents an enormous food resource.

The latest research indicates the possibility of exploitation of the same and conversion to other purposes. However, the disturbance of the "krill" population can lead to serious ecological consequences. (Paul Johnston, February 2009) Krill are small, shrimp-like crustaceans that form massive swarms in the Southern Ocean. They are a key component of the Antarctic food web, as they feed on phytoplankton and are preyed upon by fish, penguins, seals, and whales.

Krill population dynamics are influenced by various environmental factors, such as temperature, sea ice, ocean currents, and food availability. Climate change, fishing, and predation can also affect the abundance and distribution of krill.

Changes in the krill population can have cascading effects on the Antarctic ecosystem. For example, a decline in krill biomass could reduce the food supply for higher trophic levels, leading to starvation, reduced reproduction, and population decline of krill predators. Conversely, an increase in krill biomass could intensify the grazing pressure on phytoplankton, leading to depletion of primary production and reduced carbon export to the deep ocean. This could affect the biogeochemical cycles and climate feedbacks of the Southern Ocean.

Therefore, it is important to monitor and understand the factors that regulate the krill population and their impacts on the Antarctic ecosystem. This can help to develop effective conservation and management strategies for this valuable natural resource

Research missions

Every year in Antarctica about 4000 people from 27 countries live and work in research stations. Out of about 50 permanent stations, only ¾ operate during the year. Each station represents its own community in which scientific projects are carried out. Each of them is equipped with work space, kitchens, medical rooms and food reserves.

Today, they are all connected by satellite links. The largest base is McMurdo, an American base that accepts 250 people during the winter and about 1000 in the summer. Keeping these bases alive requires good planning. The ships and planes that supply the research stations with everything they need arrive in the summer. During winter, night and bad weather conditions prevail and this means that the bases are practically cut off from the rest of the world.

To undertake experiments and research scientists have to carry out field work away from the research station. Many of those activities are related to working in summer weather conditions when it is a little warmer and the day is much longer.

On land, you travel with snowmobiles, tractors, snowmobiles, while you travel by air with airplanes, helicopters. Camping is done with tents. Vehicles as well as food must be stored in separate closed rooms due to increased infrared radiation and severe weather conditions. In summer it leads to tire damage. With technological advances in nutrition, clothing, and advancements in transportation and communications, team members are well equipped and ready to face the harsh conditions. However, even in summer the weather can change and get stuck in one of the Antarctic storms.

To persevere in a regular mission, people need to be

physically fit and each person needs at least 3500 calories per day, all because of the energy he spends on warming up, moving, etc. Scientific and research missions, in addition to field work in the field, also require a research mission under the surface of the ice sheet, that is, the fulfillment of missions by diving, and this is a potentially dangerous activity that can only be faced by qualified and experienced divers. One of the hardest things in Antarctica, even though it's "funny" is finding the courage to defecate in an ice storm, special windproof toilets are made to solve that problem. However, those missions are based on common solidarity and teamwork in which everyone plays an essential element of the common good for humanity.

International cooperation in Antarctic research and governance is vital for the preservation and understanding of this unique region. Antarctica is a natural reserve devoted to peace and science, where military activity is banned and territorial claims are suspended. The Antarctic Treaty System (ATS) is the main framework for the management and regulation of Antarctic activities, based on the principles of environmental protection, scientific research, and information exchange.

The ATS consists of the Antarctic Treaty and several related agreements, such as the Protocol on Environmental Protection, the Convention on the Conservation of Antarctic Marine Living Resources, and the Convention on the Regulation of Antarctic Mineral Resource Activities. The ATS has been signed by 54 countries, representing about two-thirds of the world's population.

Scientific research is one of the main objectives and benefits of international cooperation in Antarctica. The Scientific Committee on Antarctic Research (SCAR) is an intergovernmental body that promotes, initiates, and coordinates scientific research in Antarctica and provides scientific advice to the ATS. SCAR has members from 31 countries and covers various disciplines, such as geology, biology, meteorology, oceanography, glaciology, and astronomy. SCAR also fosters collaboration among scientists from different countries and institutions, supports capacity building and education, and facilitates data sharing and standardization.

International cooperation in Antarctica also contributes to global challenges, such as climate change, biodiversity conservation, and sustainable development. Antarctica is a key component of the Earth system, influencing and responding to global processes such as ocean circulation, atmospheric circulation, carbon cycle, and sea level rise. Antarctica also hosts unique ecosystems and species that are adapted to extreme conditions and provide valuable insights into evolution, physiology, ecology, and biotechnology. Moreover, Antarctica is a source of natural resources that may have economic potential in the future, but also pose environmental risks and ethical dilemmas. Therefore, international cooperation in Antarctica is essential to monitor and understand the changes occurring in the region and their impacts on the rest of the world, as well as to ensure that any human activities are conducted in a responsible and precautionary manner.

American research missions

The American Antarctic mission is organized through three major American research stations, namely McMurdo, Amundsen Scott South Station and Palmer. The American mission has invested a lot of funds and the latest technological and technical equipment, thus placing it first in the supremacy of land and other operations carried out in Antarctica.

The American mission in Antarctica dates back to the late 19th century, when explorers such as Charles Wilkes and Richard E. Byrd led expeditions to the continent. Since then, the United States has been involved in various scientific, military, and logistical activities in Antarctica, especially during the International Geophysical Year (1957-1958) and the Operation Deep Freeze (1955-1956), which established permanent bases and conducted the first flights over the South Pole.

The United States Antarctic Program (USAP) is the current framework for coordinating and managing all U.S. activities in Antarctica, in accordance with the Antarctic Treaty System. The USAP is funded by the National Science Foundation (NSF) and supported by various federal agencies, such as the Department of State, the Department of Defense, the National Oceanic and Atmospheric Administration, and the National Aeronautics and Space Administration.

The USAP operates three year-round stations (McMurdo, Amundsen-Scott South Pole, and Palmer), two research vessels (Laurence M. Gould and Nathaniel B. Palmer), and several field camps and seasonal facilities. The USAP also provides logistical support to other countries and international organizations that conduct research in Antarctica.

Some of the major scientific achievements of the USAP include: discovering new species of plants, animals, and microorganisms; measuring the thickness and movement of ice sheets; detecting neutrinos from distant sources; monitoring climate change and ozone depletion; studying the effects of extreme environments on human physiology and psychology; and contributing to international collaborations such as the Antarctic Treaty Consultative Meeting (ATCM), the Scientific Committee on Antarctic Research (SCAR), and the Intergovernmental Panel on Climate Change (IPCC).

The USAP has invested a lot of funds and the latest technological and technical equipment to carry out its mission in Antarctica. According to the NSF budget request for fiscal year 2022, the USAP requested $465 million for Antarctic sciences, $295 million for Antarctic infrastructure and logistics, and $19 million for polar environment, health, and safety. Some of the recent or ongoing projects funded by the USAP include: upgrading the McMurdo Station facilities; modernizing the South Pole Station; developing new aircrafts, vehicles, and communication systems; deploying autonomous underwater vehicles and gliders; installing new telescopes and radars; and supporting innovative experiments such as IceCube Neutrino Observatory, Long Duration Balloon Program, Antarctic Search for Meteorites Program, and Antarctic Impulsive Transient Antenna.

The USAP plays a leading role in Antarctic research and governance, as well as in promoting Antarctica's status as a continent reserved for peace and science. The USAP also fosters international cooperation and exchange with other countries and organizations that share its interests and values in Antarctica. The USAP aims to advance scientific knowledge, protect the environment, enhance human welfare, and inspire future generations.

McMurdo Station

McMurdo Station is a United States Antarctic research station on the south tip of Ross Island, which is in the New Zealand-claimed Ross Dependency on the shore of McMurdo Sound in Antarctica. It is operated by the United States through the United States Antarctic Program (USAP), a branch of the National Science Foundation.

The station is the largest community in Antarctica. The population at McMurdo Station consists of scientists, contract workers, and other government and non-government organizations, and the number varies from 130 to 1,100 personnel . That figure depends on the time of year as well as on the activities related to scientific and constructive endeavors. The McMurdo facility or base was established in 1955 and has been operating for 147 days at full capacity. McMurdo Station is the land, sea and air base at the South Pole and all West Antarctic camps. McMurdo Station is not just a research station, but also a living and working community that has evolved over the years.

The station was originally built by the U.S. Navy as part of Operation Deep Freeze, a military and scientific project to establish a permanent presence in Antarctica. Since then, the station has been expanded and modernized to accommodate the growing number of scientists, support staff and visitors who come to McMurdo every year.

The station consists of more than 85 buildings that serve various functions, such as laboratories, offices, dormitories, dining halls, recreation facilities, medical clinics, power plants, water treatment plants, warehouses and workshops. The buildings are connected by above-ground pipes and cables that provide water, electricity, sewage and communication services. The station also has a harbor, landing strips on sea ice and shelf ice, and a helicopter pad that enable the transportation of people and cargo to and from McMurdo.

The station is designed to be self-sufficient and adaptable to the harsh Antarctic environment. The buildings are insulated and heated to keep the occupants comfortable and safe from the extreme cold. The station also has backup generators and emergency shelters in case of power outages or severe weather. The station recycles and reduces its waste as much as possible to minimize its environmental impact. The station also follows strict protocols to prevent the introduction of non-native species or contaminants to Antarctica.

McMurdo Station is not only a place of scientific discovery, but also a place of cultural diversity and social interaction. The station hosts people from different countries, backgrounds and disciplines who share a common interest in Antarctica. The station offers various activities and events to foster a sense of community and well-being among its residents, such as sports, arts, music, education, entertainment and celebrations. The station also maintains contact with the outside world through phone, email, internet and satellite TV.

McMurdo Station is a remarkable example of human ingenuity and cooperation in one of the most remote and challenging places on Earth. It is a testament to the value and importance of Antarctic research for advancing our knowledge and understanding of our planet.

It houses research centers for the Erebus volcano, oceanic and other wildlife research, as well as other mineral and ore research centers and associations. The center itself, which is more like a small town, was built and upgraded according to the needs of the base and research.

Amundsen-Scott Station

The new station has been operational since 2008 and represents in some way an artistic and technological miracle. It is built on the basis of extensive research, future needs and increased human protection. Because the station is located near the magnetic South Pole itself, it is only accessible for 100 days during the summer and supports 250 people, of which 50 stay during the winter.

Amundsen-Scott Station is the most isolated and inhospitable human outpost on Earth. It is located at the geographic South Pole, where the temperature can drop below -80°C and the sun rises and sets only once a year. The station is named after the two explorers who first reached the pole in 1911 and 1912, Ronald Amundsen and Robert Falcon Scott.

The station was first established in 1956 as part of the International Geophysical Year, a global scientific initiative to study the Earth's natural phenomena. Since then, the station has been rebuilt and relocated several times to cope with the shifting and accumulating ice, as well as to accommodate the growing number of scientists and support staff who conduct research at the pole.

The current station, which has been operational since 2008, is the fourth and most advanced version of Amundsen-Scott. It is a modular structure that consists of eight interconnected buildings that rest on adjustable hydraulic columns above the snow surface. The station can provide people with comfortable living and working spaces, such as laboratories, offices, bedrooms, bathrooms, kitchens, dining halls, lounges, gyms, libraries and medical facilities.

The station is also equipped with state-of-the-art technology and systems that enable it to function efficiently and sustainably in the harsh Antarctic environment. The station generates its own power from three diesel generators that run on jet fuel delivered by aircraft from McMurdo Station.

The station also uses renewable energy sources, such as solar panels and wind turbines, to supplement its power supply. The station recycles its water from melted snow and ice, and treats its wastewater before discharging it into deep boreholes. The station also minimizes its waste production and transports it back to McMurdo for disposal or recycling.

The station is a hub of scientific research and discovery in various fields, such as astronomy, astrophysics, meteorology, climatology, glaciology, geophysics and biology. The station hosts several instruments and experiments that take advantage of the unique conditions at the pole, such as the clear sky, the stable atmosphere, the low interference and the high altitude. Some of the notable projects at the station include the South Pole Telescope, which observes the cosmic microwave background radiation; the IceCube Neutrino Observatory, which detects high-energy neutrinos from outer space; and the Atmospheric Research Observatory, which monitors the ozone layer and greenhouse gases.

Amundsen-Scott Station is a remarkable feat of engineering and science that showcases human creativity and curiosity in exploring and understanding our world. It is a tribute to the legacy and spirit of the pioneers who first ventured to the bottom of the world.

It can be accessed by air but more recently by land from McMurdo Station. The maintenance of this station is of the utmost importance to the American mission.

Palmer Station

Palmer Station began its operational use in 1968. It is the smallest of these three permanent bases and can accommodate up to 45 people in summer and 15 people in winter. All research is limited to only a few kilometers from the base and it is difficult to access due to the inaccessible terrain.

It is even difficult to access for icebreakers due to numerous rocky areas. Due to the difficult condition of this base, it always needs effective maintenance. Palmer Station is a United States research station in Antarctica located on Anvers Island, off the coast of the Antarctic Peninsula. It is the only US station located north of the Antarctic Circle. The station was named after Nathaniel B. Palmer, who may have been the first American to see Antarctica in 1820.

The station is situated on a protected harbor on the southwestern coast of Anvers Island, surrounded by scenic mountains and glaciers. The station consists of two major buildings and three small ones, plus two large fuel tanks, a helicopter pad and a dock. The station can accommodate up to 44 people in summer and 13 people in winter.

The station is a prime location for biological studies of the rich marine ecosystem that thrives in the waters around Anvers Island. The station has a large and well-equipped laboratory and sea water aquaria, where scientists can observe and experiment with various organisms, such as algae, plankton, krill, fish, penguins, seals and whales. The station is also part of the Long Term Ecological Research

(LTER) network, which monitors the long-term changes in the Antarctic environment and climate.

In addition to biology, the station also supports research in other fields, such as oceanography, meteorology, glaciology, astronomy and astrophysics. The station operates in conjunction with a research ship, the R/V Laurence M.Gould, which provides transportation and additional facilities for scientific exploration.

Palmer Station is a unique and valuable outpost for scientific discovery and education in Antarctica. It is also a place of cultural diversity and social interaction, where people from different countries and backgrounds work together and share their experiences in one of the most remote and beautiful places on Earth.

In addition to these bases, there are 50 other research sites that are active during the summer and are accessible by helicopter, ski equipment, and even Hercules C-130 transport planes. The most visited research site is Dry Valley near McMurdo, categorized as the driest and windiest desert on Earth, a place beneath which lie vast glacial lakes frozen beneath the ice surface.

The equipment used by American bases includes research ships, as well as several icebreakers for transporting equipment and people, that is, large means of transport, including transport planes, helicopters, and snowmobiles. The transportation from McMurdo to the Amundsen Scott station was previously only possible by air, but in recent years, due to the need to transport a larger load, it takes place by land, which takes 45 days.[Report of the US Antarctic program Blue ribbon panel. Washington DC 2012] Instead of using fuel, the US mission has recently been focusing on using alternative energy sources, such as wind turbines, which will save on the costs of transportation and purchasing oil, and here we also look at the environmental security of Antarctica.

In addition to basic transportation difficulties, the American mission also faced communication problems, which is why satellites were also engaged. Through its satellites, NASA is trying to maximize data transmission as well as the duration of the transmission, and lately serious attempts have been made to transmit the Internet in real time due to the needs of scientists.

The safety and health of the US mission is at the highest level. The greatest danger is from infectious diseases, as in 2008 there was an example of influenza infection among 330 members of the staff of McMurdo Station, which is approximately 48% of the total number engaged on the base. Each sick person not only represents a loss of work effectiveness, but also represents a burden on the rest of the people of the community.

The conditions for a better success of the American mission, according to the American experts provided to the White House, depend on several factors:

-Internet transmission that needs to be improved and modernized;

-Improving the transportation system to Palmer Station;

-Reconstruction of aerial access to McMurdo due to snowmelt;

-Fire hazard due to inadequate grounding;

-Replacement of obsolete equipment and the polar fleet of ships;

-Improved logistics and air supply;

-Improved protection through quarantine;

-International cooperation;

-Etc.

The US Antarctic mission is the largest and most organized of all missions. We will list the other more important missions in Antarctica in brief.

Russian Antarctic Mission

The Russian mission in Antarctica is a continuation of the scientific and exploratory activities that began under the Soviet Union in 1955. The mission is organized by the Soviet Antarctic Expedition (SAE), which was renamed the Russian Antarctic Expedition (RAE) in 1991 after the collapse of the Soviet Union.

The RAE is a branch of the Arctic and Antarctic Research Institute (AARI), which is a federal state budgetary institution that conducts research and provides services related to the polar regions. The AARI is part of the Russian Academy of Sciences (RAS), which is the national academy of sciences and the highest scientific organization in Russia.

The RAE operates several research stations in Antarctica, some of which are open year-round and some of which are seasonal. The RAE also maintains two icebreakers, the Akademik Fyodorov and the Akademik Tryoshnikov, that transport personnel and cargo to and from Antarctica. The RAE conducts research in various fields, such as geology, glaciology, meteorology, oceanography, biology, medicine and astronomy.

The RAE also participates in international scientific cooperation and exchange with other countries and organizations involved in Antarctic research.

The RAE is one of the oldest and most active national missions in Antarctica. It has made significant contributions to the exploration and understanding of the Antarctic continent and its surrounding oceans. The RAE has also played an important role in the development and implementation of the Antarctic Treaty System, which regulates the peaceful use and protection of Antarctica.

The first Russian Mirny base was established in 1956. A second base named Vostok was built in the interior of Antarctica right near the South Magnetic Pole. Six more permanent bases were established in that period, including: Novolazarevskaya (1961), Modozhnaya (1963), Bellingshausen (1968), Leningradskaya (1971), Russkaya (1980) and Progress (1988).

Vostok station

The Vostok station is located in the coldest place on the planet. The coldest temperature known and confirmed on Earth was measured there (-89.2° C).

Thus, the Russian mission is positioned mostly in the eastern part of Antarctica. About 25 scientists stay in the Vostok base during the summer, and the number can drop to 13 during the winter. In similar conditions, only the American Amundsen-Scott survives at the geographic South Pole. British and Russian scientists near this base discovered and later confirmed the existence of Lake Vostok, which lies about 4 km below the surface of the Antarctic ice sheet. Lake Vostok was finally reached by drilling, in February 2012, at a depth of 3345 m, and in doing so, reached the surface of the waters of the frozen lake, for which there is still no new information. It can be said that several factors make the surroundings of the Vostok base one of the most inhabitable places on Earth.

Those factors are: almost complete lack of moisture in the air, winds that blow continuously at speeds of up to 90 km/h, lack of oxygen due to a high altitude of 3500 meters, higher ionization of the air, polar night that lasts an incredible 130 days and twilight from 80 days during the summer period, therefore adaptation, i.e. acclimatization in such conditions can last from one week to two months, during which frequent headaches, temporary blindness, nosebleeds, unexpected increase in blood pressure, insomnia, loss of appetite, vomiting, muscle pain and weight loss. All this indicates that such extraordinary occurrences may play an aggravating role in conquering the Antarctic landmass in some future resource struggle.

In addition to the Vostok station, the Mirni station is also more active, housing 160 people in the summer and about 60 people in the winter.

Other Antarctic missions

China participates with 3 polar bases in Antarctica and has invested about 60 million dollars to improve its polar research centers.

The most famous are the Changcheng (Great Wall) station, established in 1985 with a total capacity of 40 people, and immediately after, in 1989, the Zhongshan station was built. Both stations are in the coastal part of Antarctica. This year, through its icebreaker Juelong, it is trying to establish a new, fourth station in a row.

These stations allow China to conduct scientific investigations on various topics, such as glaciology, geology, marine biology, and atmospheric sciences1

The report also revealed that China is building a fifth station on Inexpressible Island near the Ross Sea, which is expected to be completed by 2024. The new station will include an observatory with a satellite ground station, a wharf for icebreaker ships, and a helicopter pad4

The expansion of China's Antarctic infrastructure has raised some concerns among western governments, who worry that China may use its stations for military or strategic purposes, such as surveillance, resource exploitation, or maritime access4 Under the Antarctic Treaty, which China signed in 1983, all activities on the continent must be for peaceful purposes only, and military activities are prohibited. However, some analysts argue that China's growing presence in Antarctica could challenge the existing governance system and pose potential risks to the environment and security of the region.

Other significant Antarctic missions are the Australian, British, Argentine and Chilean. They all participate with independent or mixed staff.

Political agreements for Antarctica

The Antarctic Treaty was signed on December 1, 1959, and entered into force on June 23, 1961. It is also the main document that applies to all Antarctic misunderstandings and legislation between the signatory countries.

Antarctic Treaty as part of The Antarctic Treaty System (Antarctic Treaty System) regulates international relations with respect to Antarctica, the only uninhabited continent. The definition of Antarctica in this treaty includes all lands south of 60° horizontal. For now, 50 countries of the world are signatories and they have banned all military activities in that agreement. It is also the only agreement signed during the Cold War, in which military engagement is prohibited, that is, the first arms control was established.[Encyclopedia Britannica Inc., 15-th edn., 1992, Vol, 1, p.439]

The first signatory countries are Australia, Argentina, Belgium, Chile, France, Japan, New Zealand, Norway, South Africa, USSR, Great Britain and the USA.

These countries alone had about 50 stations operating at the time. The following topics are defined in the agreement:

-The area will be used only for peaceful purposes;

-The use of military tests and activities is prohibited, but military equipment and people may be used for scientific purposes;

-Free exchange of information on Antarctic discoveries;

-The agreement does not respect new territorial claims

or deny existing ones.

-Ban on nuclear testing and waste;

-This includes all land and ice areas, but not waters south of 60°;

-The signatory countries are obliged to allow control by independent observers, both from the air and from the ground, and to introduce their personnel;

-All disagreements should be resolved peacefully and eventually the International Court of Justice will be involved.

In fact, this agreement should have the main goal of preventing Antarctica from becoming a war zone, but in the long term, the agreement did not completely prevent the participation of military personnel, except to minimize the danger.

Apart from this agreement, numerous other agreements were signed, we will list the most important ones:

-Treaty on the Conservation of Antarctic Flora and Fauna (1964);

-Antarctic Seal Conservation Treaty (1972);

-Convention on the Regulation of Antarctic Mineral Activities (1988);

-Protocol on Environmental Protection to the Antarctic Treaty (1991);

*It is interesting that the convention on Antarctic mineral activities has not yet entered into force, although it was signed in 1988.

*The Antarctic Treaty System annually holds meetings under the name Antarctic Treaty Consultative Meetings (ATCM) .

*Of all the signatory member countries, only 28 have the right to decide.

*16 signatory countries have shown particular interest in the scientific research that is being carried out.

In Antarctica there is still an area[Wright, Minturn, "The Ownership of Antarctica, Its living and Mineral

Resources", Journal of Law and the Environment (1987)] that is 90° west and 150° east, that is not yet claimed by any country. Also the Antarctic Treaty prevents that. So far, several countries have claims for their territories on Antarctic, namely Argentina, Australia, New Zealand, Norway, Germany, France and Chile.

Russia and the United States have retained the right to claim ownership of their territories. The Antarctic Treaty is often seen as representative of the common heritage of human principles.

Each country in its bases has its own legal system inherited from the countries from which they originate. For example, the United States has sent sheriffs to regulate legal procedures.

Struggle for resources in Antarctica

A great power is a state that is recognized as having the ability to influence world events. Great powers, by this definition, should possess military and economic power as well as diplomatic influence that will cause smaller states to take those views into account before taking their own actions.

Great powers are states that have the ability and the willingness to shape the international system according to their interests and values. Great powers have three main characteristics that distinguish them from other states: military and economic power, diplomatic influence and global reach.

Military and economic power are the material foundations of great power status. Great powers have strong and capable armed forces that can project power across regions and continents, as well as deter or defeat potential adversaries. Great powers also have large and dynamic economies that can sustain their military spending, support their allies and partners, and compete with their rivals.

Diplomatic influence is the political dimension of great power status. Great powers have a network of allies, partners and clients that share their strategic goals and cooperate with them on various issues. Great powers also have a voice and a vote in international organizations and institutions that shape the norms and rules of the international system. Great powers can use their diplomatic influence to persuade, coerce or reward other states to follow their lead or accept their preferences.

Global reach is the geographic scope of great power status. Great powers have interests and involvement in all regions of the world, not just in their own neighborhood. Great powers can affect and be affected by events and developments that occur far from their borders. Great powers can also mobilize their military, economic and diplomatic resources to address global challenges and opportunities.

Great powers, therefore, are states that have the capacity and the ambition to shape the international system in their favor. They are not only concerned with their own security and prosperity, but also with the stability and order of the world as a whole. They are not only reactive to external threats and opportunities, but also proactive in creating and changing them. They are not only followers of existing rules and norms, but also makers of new ones.

Formally, such status is recognized by the Security Council in the United Nations.[TV Paul, James J. Wirtz, Michel Fortmann (2005). Balance of Power. United States of America: State University of New York Press, 2005. pp. 59, 282. ISBN 0791464016. p.59] According to it, the Great Powers after the Cold War are: USA, Britain, China, France, Germany, Japan, Russia and China. Apart from these forces, the countries closest to Antarctica are also included today, namely Argentina and Australia.the exploitation of non-living resources is prohibited by the Protocol on Environmental Protection to the Antarctic Treaty (also known as the Madrid Protocol), which bans any activity relating to mineral resources other than scientific research. The protocol also imposes strict environmental standards and obligations for any human activity in Antarctica. Moreover, the exploitation of non-living resources is hampered by the harsh climate, remote location and high costs of operating in Antarctica.

Great powers have different motivations and interests in accessing and exploiting Antarctica's resources. Some great powers may seek to secure their energy security or economic growth by tapping into Antarctica's untapped reserves of oil, gas or minerals. Some great powers may seek to enhance their scientific prestige or innovation by conducting cutting-edge research on Antarctica's unique natural phenomena or biological diversity. Some great powers may seek to assert their political influence or strategic advantage by establishing their presence or claims in Antarctica or its surrounding waters.

However, great powers also face different constraints and challenges in pursuing their interests in Antarctica's resources. They have to abide by the rules and norms of the Antarctic Treaty System (ATS), which governs the peaceful use and cooperation in Antarctica among its 54 signatory states. They have to balance their national interests with their international responsibilities and reputation as responsible actors in the global community. They have to deal with the uncertainties and risks of operating in a complex and dynamic environment that is subject to rapid changes due to climate change and human activities.

Therefore, the struggle for resources in Antarctica by great powers is not a simple or straightforward matter. It is a multifaceted and dynamic issue that involves legal, environmental, economic, scientific, political and strategic dimensions. It is also an issue that requires cooperation, coordination and compromise among great powers and other stakeholders to ensure the protection and preservation of Antarctica as a natural reserve devoted to peace and science.

As we have already said, the Antarctic Treaty entered into force in 1961 and with that agreement the security and "permanent" peace and demilitarization of Antarctica was achieved. The contract does not have a restrictive time period, but it may be canceled in the near future, and several factors indicate this. First of those factors is that Antarctica is the last place in the world as an untouched reservoir of mineral resources in the world.[Radio Free Europe/Radio Liberty, July 27, 2007] If the expansion of the Australian territory is formalized, this could disrupt the established legal mechanisms that have already been seriously disrupted by the the war in Ukraine and the claim of sovereign countries not to be recognized by international borders. Similar to Antarctica, the division of the Arctic, which already includes Russia and Canada, may occur earlier.[Russian Information Agency Novosti, April 24, 2008]

There are already announcements from Britain that it will submit a claim to expand its territories in Antarctica by a million square kilometers and will also submit four other claims, including the island of South Georgia and the Falklands Islands.[Reuters, October 7, 2007.] Since 1962, the British Antarctic Territory had been a dependency of the Falkland Islands and the implications of that war with Argentina in 1982 probably arose from the loss of a base connecting Britain directly to Antarctica, South Georgia and the South Sandwich Islands. Thus, at the United Nations, Britain does not hide its ambitions to expand the zone that covers the vast area around British Antarctica along the South Pole. The formalization of this plan was announced in October, 2007.

The British Antarctic Territory (BAT) is a sector of Antarctica claimed by the United Kingdom as one of its 14 British Overseas Territories. It is the UK's largest overseas territory, with a land area of 1,709,400 sq. km. The BAT comprises the region south of 60°S latitude and between longitudes 20°W and 80°W, forming a wedge shape that extends to the South Pole. The area includes the South Orkney Islands, the South Shetland Islands, the Antarctic Peninsula and adjacent islands, and mainland Antarctica extending to the South Pole.

The UK's claim to this portion of the Antarctic dates back to letters patent of 1908 and 1917. However, all territorial sovereignty claims to Antarctica are held in abeyance under Article IV of the Antarctic Treaty 1959, which states that no acts or activities taking place while the treaty is in force shall constitute a basis for asserting, supporting or denying a claim to territorial sovereignty in Antarctica. The UK has ratified the treaty and is one of the 12 original signatories.

The BAT is administered in London by the Polar Regions Department of the Foreign, Commonwealth & Development Office. The BAT has a Commissioner, a Deputy Commissioner and an Administrator who are responsible for overseeing the governance and management of the territory. The BAT also has its own flag, coat of arms, motto, anthem, currency, postcode and internet domain23

The BAT is inhabited by the staff of research and support stations operated by the British Antarctic Survey (BAS) and other countries. There are no native or permanent residents. The BAS conducts scientific research in various fields, such as biology, geology, glaciology, meteorology, oceanography and astronomy. The BAS also maintains historical sites and monuments in the BAT that commemorate the exploration and discovery of Antarctica.

The BAT is subject to international agreements and regulations that aim to protect the Antarctic environment and promote peaceful cooperation among Antarctic states. These include the Protocol on Environmental Protection to the Antarctic Treaty (also known as the Madrid Protocol), which bans any activity relating to mineral resources other than scientific research; the Convention on the Conservation of Antarctic Marine Living Resources (CCAMLR), which regulates fishing activities in Antarctic waters; and the Agreement on the Conservation of Albatrosses and Petrels (ACAP), which aims to reduce threats to seabirds in Antarctica.

The BAT is a unique and valuable part of the UK's overseas territories that contributes to the advancement of knowledge and understanding of Antarctica and its global role.

Reactions to British claims

Immediately, nations that are geographically much closer to the South Pole filed complaints arguing that Britain's territorial claims were contrary to the spirit of the Antarctic Treaty, to which Britain is a signatory, which prevents the exploitation of oil, gas and minerals, except of what scientific discoveries entail. Alarms were immediately sounded on the other side of the globe, where the Chinese People's Daily reported that Antarctica has become a hot spot lately and that Argentina and Chile will discuss the South Pole situation and how to boycott Britain's demands.[People's Daily, December 4, 2007]

At the same time, the same source presents data that Antarctica hides 500 billion tons of known coal reserves. Also, the thin ice on the surface of Antarctica covers 75% of the world's known reserves of drinking water. It can be said that the South Pole can feed the whole world with its fish stock as well as its fresh water.

The value of the South Pole can be said to lie not only in its economic, but also its strategic position. We saw that from Nazi Germany's attempt to use that strategic position in World War II.

It should not be forgotten that the number one air force in world is the US Air Force. But if the Antarctic Treaty is not respected, the cold South Pole could turn into a fierce battleground where several players would play a key role.

Therefore, immediately after Britain's announcement, Chilean Minister Jose Goni and the head of Chilean aviation visited the South Pole and announced the opening of a naval base in 2008. Apart from the military base, Chile also announced the opening of two military bases that would demonstrate Chile's presence in the region.

Canadian newspapers wondered why anyone would even need to claim territory for themselves on the coast of Antarctica, on an uninhabited frozen island that was conquered only 100 years ago? Surely the motivation lies deep in the seabed, minerals, oil and gas.[Toronto Star, November 18, 2007]

Russia also reacted to the British claim to the territory and said: "Being one of the nations that made the greatest contribution to the development of the Antarctic Treaty and scientific development, this country is constantly working against the idea of dividing Antarctica on the basis of unilateral territorial claims and that's why he doesn't recognize them."[Reuters, October 7, 2007]

Never before, since the Golden Age of Empires, has Britain claimed so much territory, but with that empire gone, Antarctica has become a battleground for world powers competing on several fronts to secure the oil-rich territory.

Researcher Tanya Thompson explains what it is all about:

"Britain is preparing territorial claims to tens of thousands of square kilometers of the Atlantic Ocean around the Falkland and Rock Islands in the hope of annexing oil and gas fields lying on the ocean floor."[The Scotsman, October 23, 2007]

In doing so, she cites data that the war over the Falklands, which took place more than 30 years ago, is due to oil, which, according to some seismic measurements, may have more than 60 billion barrels under the ocean floor. And indeed, it is inevitable that, apart from these events related to the Falklands War in 1982, the Falklands is also an uninhabited place, this did not prevent Britain and Argentina from many, including Environment Minister Peter Garrett who claims that experts have confirmed possible rise in the level of all seas and oceans by as much as 6 meters by 2100.[Global Research, May

16, 2009]

The Antarctic Treaty reads: "It is in the interest of mankind that Antarctica should continue forever to be used only for peaceful purposes and not become a scene or object of international disturbance, therefore Antarctica should be used only for peaceful purposes." Therefore, all measures of a military nature, such as the establishment of military bases and fortifications, military maneuvers, as well as the testing of any type of weapon, should be prohibited." Massively militarized Australia, in its self-proclaimed Antarctic territory

Australia and its ambitions

In addition to Britain, Australia, its former colony, also shows special interest in Antarctica. With this, the majority of Western Powers and their allies show an increased military interest in greater control of the world's resources. In 2008, in an unprecedented event, Australia was awarded 2.5 million square kilometers by a United Nations commission, formalizing control over a territory as large as "five Frances" as noted by the Australian Government's Minister for Resources, Martin Ferguson.[Agence France-Presse, April 21, 2008.] This territory was not in Antarctica, but in the seabed off the coast of Australia, extending its continental shelf and exclusive economic zone.

The UN commission was the Commission on the Limits of the Continental Shelf (CLCS), a body of experts established under the United Nations Convention on the Law of the Sea (UNCLOS). UNCLOS is an international treaty that defines the rights and responsibilities of states in their use of the world's oceans. UNCLOS allows coastal states to claim a continental shelf up to 200 nautical miles from their shorelines, or beyond that limit if they can prove that the seabed is a natural prolongation of their land territory.

Australia ratified UNCLOS in 1994 and submitted its claim to extend its continental shelf to the CLCS in 2004. The claim was based on extensive scientific and legal research conducted by Geo-science Australia and other agencies. The claim covered 65 areas off Australia's coast, totaling about 3.37 million square kilometers. The CLCS examined and approved most of Australia's claim in 2008, granting it sovereign rights over an additional 2.5 million square kilometers of seabed. This was the largest area ever awarded to a single country by the CLCS.

The extended continental shelf gives Australia exclusive rights to explore and exploit the natural resources of the seabed, such as oil, gas, minerals and biological resources. It also gives Australia responsibilities to protect and preserve the marine environment and to cooperate with other states and international organizations in managing the seabed resources. The extended continental shelf does not affect the rights of other states to use the water column above the seabed for navigation, fishing or other purposes.

The awarding of 2.5 million square kilometers by a UN commission was a historic achievement for Australia that recognized its geographic and geological features and enhanced its maritime jurisdiction. It also demonstrated Australia's commitment to the rule of law and peaceful settlement of disputes in accordance with UNCLOS.

It will cause a boom in the discovery and use of underwater oil and gas reserves in that territory that includes and runs around the coast of Antarctica. With this, Australia de facto becomes the first country to be granted the right to rule the ocean near Antarctica. This information would not be interesting if it were not also pointed to the opinion of the analyst Dmitri Yefstafiev from the Center for Political Studies in Moscow, who indicates that such formalization can lead to a struggle for resources first at the North Pole, and then to a struggle for resources at the South Pole.

Just one year later, in 2008, Australia announced a $72 billion project to increase military spending and the construction of its military and naval fleet. Intentionally or unintentionally included in the procurement: 12 state-of-the-art submarine "hunters" on ships, three destroyer interceptors each equipped with state-of-the-art "tomahawk" missiles, then 100 US F-35 fighter jets. This could certainly be linked to the deployment of the vast area of 2.5 million kilometers that Australia now has, thereby violating the signed agreement that includes the demilitarization of the Antarctic area.

Areas of interest and territories

Four countries are directly involved in the Antarctic Ocean, namely South Africa, Chile, Australia and New Zealand, all of which are part of Western military alliances and special alliances with the United States, ie NATO. Seven countries have formal claims to Antarctic territory: three are NATO members in Europe (Britain, France and Norway), two are former British colonies (Commonwealth) in the South Pacific (Australia and New Zealand) and two are South American countries (Chile and Argentina). Argentine, British and Chilean territories overlap in some places. Peru, Russia, South Africa and the USA have reserved the right to claim their own territories in the coming period. While Brazil has oriented itself towards what is called a zone of interest in the region. Only Chile and Argentina opposed the claims made by Britain, thus demonstrating a common determination to resist unilateral action and interference. But while Chile's role is still not entirely clear, given its non-interference in the Falklands War, Argentina is already showing signs of favoring Russia.

Russia is already sending aid to Argentina's 6 bases in Antarctica, while Argentina is showing interest in buying Russian equipment and helicopters. This is proven by the larger and more frequent visits as well as the planned military exercises between the two countries. But unlike Argentina, Chile is arming itself "to the teeth" with equipment from NATO and its allies.

The Ukraine crisis has implications for Antarctica in several ways. First, it has increased the strategic importance of Antarctica as a potential source of energy, minerals and other resources that could be exploited in the future. Antarctica is estimated to have vast reserves of oil, gas, coal, iron ore, copper, gold and other minerals that could be worth trillions of dollars. However, the exploitation of these resources is currently prohibited by the Protocol on Environmental Protection to the Antarctic Treaty (also known as the Madrid Protocol), which bans any activity relating to mineral resources other than scientific research.

The protocol also imposes strict environmental standards and obligations for any human activity in Antarctica. The protocol is due to be reviewed in 2048, and some countries may seek to revise or withdraw from it in order to access Antarctica's resources3

Second, the Ukraine crisis has increased the political influence of Antarctica as a platform for demonstrating national interests, capabilities and presence in the region. Antarctica is subject to overlapping territorial claims by seven countries: Argentina, Australia, Chile, France, New Zealand, Norway and the United Kingdom. These claims are not recognized by most other countries and are held in abeyance under Article IV of the Antarctic Treaty 1959, which states that no acts or activities taking place while the treaty is in force shall constitute a basis for asserting, supporting or denying a claim to territorial sovereignty in Antarctica. However, some claimant countries may seek to strengthen or expand their claims in response to the Ukraine crisis, either by increasing their scientific research, infrastructure development or military presence in Antarctica, or by challenging or contesting the claims of other countries.

Third, the Ukraine crisis has increased the security risks of Antarctica as a potential target or venue for military actions or provocations by hostile actors. Antarctica is governed by the Antarctic Treaty System (ATS), which is a set of international agreements that regulate the peaceful use and cooperation in Antarctica among its 54 signatory states. The ATS prohibits any measures of a military nature in Antarctica, such as the establishment of military bases or fortifications, the carrying out of military maneuvers or exercises, or the testing of any type of weapons. However, some countries may seek to circumvent or violate these rules in order to gain an advantage or challenge an adversary in Antarctica. For example, some countries may use their civilian research stations or vessels as cover for conducting military activities or intelligence operations in Antarctica. Some countries may also use their military assets or personnel to support their civilian activities or protect their interests in Antarctica. Some countries may even use their nuclear weapons or missiles to threaten or attack targets in Antarctica or its surrounding waters.

Therefore, Antarctica is not immune from the effects of the Ukraine crisis. It is a continent that faces multiple challenges and opportunities from great powers that have different motivations and interests in accessing and exploiting its resources, influencing its politics and ensuring its security. It is also a continent that requires cooperation, coordination and compromise among great powers and other stakeholders to ensure its protection and preservation as a natural reserve devoted to peace and science.

Conclusion

An accelerated melting of the ice has been observed in Antarctica, and any war game and testing can cause an accelerated disruption of all environmental factors that threaten a global ecological crisis.

The heirs of the former Neo-colonialism are not resting and are once again creating fertile ground for opening a new climate in history whose mechanisms will be activated as soon as the established balance and previous agreements are disturbed. Britain, in a similar way, disturbs that balance and it is certain that Russia and China as two strong rising powers will not be left out in the making of policy towards Antarctica. Here, a huge role is played by the attitude of Argentina, which increasingly plays a counterweight to Australia.

Violation of the balance and agreements can lead to military conflicts and the same will result in unforeseeable consequences for humanity.

The Ukraine crisis has shown that Antarctica is not isolated from the geopolitical tensions and conflicts that affect the rest of the world. Great powers may seek to exploit Antarctica's resources, assert their claims, or challenge their rivals in the region, potentially violating the rules and norms that govern the peaceful use and cooperation in Antarctica.

However, such actions could have dire consequences for the Antarctic environment and the global climate. Antarctica is already facing the threat of climate change, which is causing the ice to melt at an alarming rate, raising sea levels and disrupting ecosystems. Any war game and testing in Antarctica could exacerbate this situation, causing further damage to the ice, the wildlife and the atmosphere. This could trigger a global ecological crisis that would affect not only Antarctica, but also the rest of the world. Therefore, it is imperative that great powers respect and uphold the Antarctic Treaty System, which aims to protect and preserve Antarctica as a natural reserve devoted to peace and science. It is also essential that great powers cooperate and collaborate with each other and with other stakeholders to address the common challenges and opportunities that Antarctica presents. Antarctica is a continent that belongs to no one, but to everyone.

It is a continent that requires not competition and conflict, but cooperation and compromise. It is a continent that deserves not exploitation and destruction, but protection and preservation.

Literature:

Foundation, NS (2012). More and better Science in Antarctica Through Increased Logistical Effectiveness. Washington DC: White House Office of Science and Technology.

Paul Johnston, DS (February 2009). Gambling with Krill Fisheries in the Antarctic: Large uncertainties equote with high risks. Greenpeace Research Laboratories Technical Note.

http://science1.nasa.gov

Wright, Minturn, The Ownership of Antarctica, Its living and Mineral Resources , Journal of Law and the Environment (1987)

TV Paul, James J. Wirtz, Michel Fortmann (2005). Balance of Power . United States of America: State University of New York Press, 2005

Future Science. Opportunities in Antarctica.

ABOUT THE AUTHOR

Timurlenk Chekovikj is the author of several works that explore the relationship between Islam and science, other religions and everyday life. With his short story "Implant-um" he appears in front of the public for the first time with a prose work, although he has been writing for a long time. The sci-fi novel The Merge: When the Line between AI and Humanity Blurs is his first book on this topic and probably the first serial in a row. He has a master's degree in crisis management at the Military Academy in Skopje. Researches the impacts of global threats and security. He is interested in writing and sharing news in technology, global changes and events. Focuses on geo-spatial intelligence and technological advances, as well as ethical values and history. He has an active blog and is the author of several books, academic articles and research.